Power Tools Part 1: Prayer Power

Building Foundations: A Spirit Filled Children's Church Curriculum

Pastor Tamera Kraft
Revival Fire 4 Kids Resource

Mt Zion Ridge Press
http://mtzionridgepress.com
Managing Editors: Michelle L. Levigne and Tamera Lynn Kraft
Cover Art: Tamera Lynn Kraft

ISBN: 978-1-955838-08-5

Registration and Digital Files (Available for FREE with purchase of the curriculum): Digital files (jpeg graphics, video clips, other resources) are available to anyone who purchases and registers this curriculum at no additional cost. To register, click on this link http://eepurl.com/glsELH or type it in the address box on your browser and fill out the form. We never sell or give away any information we receive.

DVD: If you prefer a DVD of Jpeg images and video clips, you may purchase it at http://mtzionridgepress.com for an additional cost.

Power Tools is a 3 part curriculum which includes these sections that can be bought together in one manual or bought separately:

- **Part 1 – Prayer Power (4 lessons on the power of prayer included in this manual)**
- Part 2 – Worship Power (4 Lessons on the power of worshipping God)
- Part 3 – Holy Spirit Power (5 lessons on how the baptism and gifts of the Holy Spirit equip you with power)

Power Tools is available in PDF download and print. Each part of *Power Tools* is available separately in PDF download or print.

All Scripture in this curriculum is from the NIV (2011) Bible unless otherwise designated.

For questions about copyright issues or other matter concerning rights for this curriculum, contact revivalfire4kids@att.net.

Building Foundations Curriculum is a Revival Fire for Kids resource. For more information about Revival Fire for Kids, check out their website at http://revivalfire4kids.net

Materials included:

Prayer Power: 4 complete downloadable lessons including 8 object lessons, 8 skits, 8 games, 4 Bible Stories, 4 memory verse activities, graphics to be used in PowerPoint slides for 8 lessons, 4 small group discussions, and optional lessons and activities. Lessons, graphics, videos, and Family Devotion Handouts will be available for immediate download.

TABLE OF CONTENTS

How To Use This Curriculum:

Scriptural Premise: God does not leave us powerless in our Christian journey. He gives us tools to empower us for everything He wants us to do. Among these power tools are prayer, worship, the baptism of the Holy Spirit, and the gifts of the Holy Spirit.

Decorations: Decorations and set design should reflect building construction with drills, saws, and power tools. If you have purchased *The Journey*, another *Building Foundations Curriculum*, you could use the decorations for *The Journey* and add power tools. You could also borrow power tools from someone and set up a power tools garage or store.

Another idea is to use a backdrop with the cover picture of *Power Tools or Power Tools* backdrop as templates for a backdrop. You can use any image included with this curriculum by projecting the image using a video projector onto a box or backdrop and drawing it. Use your creativity.

Italics: Italics are used for Scripture. They are also used in this curriculum for passages or speeches the teacher or worker may want to say in their own words. For skits, italics are only used to designate the person speaking.

Welcome:

Welcome: Each lesson will welcome the children with an introduction to that day's message.

Prayer: It's important to start each lesson with prayer.

Rules: A list of 5 Ups are included in the graphics available after registration. Rehearse the rules every week.

Theme Song: Get the kids up and moving at the beginning of every lesson with a fun theme song. Theme song that will work with this curriculum are *Jesus Prayer* by Brad G Kids, *The Lord's Prayer* by Summit Kids, or *There is Power* by Lincoln Brewster.

Memory Verse: Every lesson has a memory verse. The verse will be included in a slide and will be illustrated in three ways. You can choose to use any of these illustrations to teach the verse, or you could use all three throughout your lesson.

Memory Verse Skit: A puppet or live skit with Doctor Word is included in each lesson to introduce the Memory Verse. The person doing the skit can dress as a doctor or in scrubs. If a doctor, nurse, or medical professional attends you church, it would be great to him for your skits and have him wear his work clothes. You can also use a doctor puppet for these skits if you have a puppet team.

Memory Verse Talk: This is a short talk explaining what the verse means to the children. Memorizing God's Word is important, but it's more important for your students to know what a verse means.

Memory Verse Activity: Children learn by seeing, reading, hearing, and doing. The memory verse activity is a simple tool to help students remember the verse longer.

Game Time: A Game Time slide is included with registration for this curriculum. It isn't necessary to include a game with every week's lesson, but if you do, you should have a fun game that relates to the lessons. Game Time is the place for that. You may also want to save the game for last so, if the adult service runs long, you can play games until the parents arrive to retrieve their children.

Video Clips: *Power Tools Countdown* and video clips for some lessons are included with *Prayer Power* along with other downloadable files. A link to a Dropbox files with be sent to your email after you have registered your curriculum. *Building Foundations* doesn't provide video curriculum to teach the lessons.

1

Instead, it provides short, fun video clips to help the children remember the lesson in a fun way.

Offering: Lessons include a short talk on why children should give in the offering. You can expand the fun by having an offering contest with the boys against the girls. You can use a scale with buckets or have two offering plates and count the money. Once a month or once a quarter, have a special reward for the winning team.

Praise & Worship: Each week, a time of praise and worship is included to ready the students' hearts to hear the Word of God. This curriculum does not provide music because every church has different musical needs.

Lesson of the Week:

Skit: Two skits about each week's lesson are included. One skit uses a doctor, Doctor Word, to introduce the memory verse for the day. Another skit uses a silly character named Tyler the Power Tool Guy or Gal. These skits require few props and only two people, the leader and another worker, making them easy for even small churches to use. Doctor Word skits can be used as puppet skits if you have a puppet ministry. Tyler the Power Tool Guy or Gal could also be used with puppets but may need some modification when props are involved.

Bible Story: Each week, a Bible story is included to go with the lesson.

Object Lessons: At least two object lessons illustrate the points of each week's lesson. Resources for the object lessons are not included.

Message: A short message ties up the lesson for the day and asks for a response from the students.

Optional Resources: Optional Resources are included with object lessons and other inactive events as suggestions for additional teaching activities. The props for optional resources are not included but are easy to obtain.

Small Group Chat: Some children's ministries prefer to end each children's service with a small group chat, or they have a small group Bible study at some time during the week. Small group chat questions and activities are included for these purposes. Divide students into small groups of not more than six children. You can divide them by ages or include different ages together. Questions and instructions for activities are included to help the leader facilitate a chat with the students about the lesson. Small group sessions will help your students go home with practical applications for what they have learned.

Home Application: Each lesson will include a handout for the children to take home. Each handout will include this week's memory verse, a summary of the lesson, a Bible reading for each day, and a weekly family activity. This handout is available as a printable PDF download upon registration of this curriculum. This will be helpful guide for parents who have family devotions.

Registration and Digital Files (Available for FREE with purchase of the curriculum): Digital files (jpeg graphics, video clips, other resources) are available to anyone who purchases and registers this curriculum at no additional cost. To register, click on this link http://eepurl.com/glsELH or type it in the address box on your browser and fill out the form. We never sell or give away any information we receive.

Power Tools 1: Prayer Power Lessons

5 Finger Prayer

Matthew 6:9-13 (NKJV) *Our Father in heaven, Hallowed be Your name.*
Your kingdom come. Your will be done On earth as it is in heaven.
Give us this day our daily bread. And forgive us our debts, As we forgive our debtors.
And do not lead us into temptation, But deliver us from the evil one.
For Yours is the kingdom and the power and the glory forever. Amen.

Don't Worry - Pray

Philippians 4:6 (ICB) *"Do not worry about anything. But pray and ask God for everything you need. And when you pray, always give thanks."*

FAITH Prayer

Matthew 17:20 … *If you have faith as small as a mustard seed, you can say to this mountain, 'Move from here to there,' and it will move. Nothing will be impossible for you.*

Powerful Prayer

James 5: 16 … *The prayer of a righteous person is powerful and effective.*

Lesson 1 - 5 Finger Prayer

Focus Point: Jesus taught us how to pray.

Goal: Students will learn the Lord's Prayer model to help them prayer.

Verse of the Day: Matthew 6:9-13 (NKJV) ... *Our Father in heaven, Hallowed be Your name.*

Your kingdom come. Your will be done On earth as it is in heaven.

Give us this day our daily bread. And forgive us our debts, As we forgive our debtors.

And do not lead us into temptation, But deliver us from the evil one.

For Yours is the kingdom and the power and the glory forever. Amen.

Supplies Needed:

- doctor puppet or doctor costume for skit
- portable toolbox with various tools
- Tyler the Power Tool Guy Skit: Tyler wears a portable toolbox or toolbelt with various tools and is dressed in blue jeans and a plaid shirt, etc.
- power screwdriver
- paper plate
- bread
- lunchmeat
- lettuce
- ketchup, mustard, and other sandwich elements
- cheese
- Marker board, chalk board, or blank wall
- scotch tape
- 1 set of strips of paper or poster board
- marker board
- poster
- rock
- rubber snake
- bread
- toy fish

Opening: *Power Tools Countdown* or *Power Tools* Slide (Available free with registration of this curriculum.)

Welcome: *Welcome to Power Tools. For the next few weeks, we will learn about one of the* *most powerful tools in a Christian's life, the power of prayer. Prayer is more than saying the right words. Prayer is talking the King of Kings and Lord of Lords. Prayer is talking to God.*

Prayer: Ask a child to pray over the service.

Rules: (use rules slide) Go over the 5 Ups Rules.

Go over the *5 Ups Rules*: 1. Sit up straight. 2. Listen up. 3. Hush up. 4. Don't get up and run around or go to the bathroom. 5. Worship Up! (stand up and participate during praise and worship)

Theme or Activity Songs: Choose one of two fast moving activity or theme songs that go with the curriculum.

Game Time: Telephone (use game time slide)

Supplies Needed: none

This is the traditional game of telephone. Whisper "Our Father in Heaven. Hallowed be Your Name," in the first student's ear. Have that student whisper into the next student's ear. Continue until it reaches the last student. Have that student announce what he heard.

When playing telephone, it's important to speak clearly and listen carefully. That's true in prayer too. God wants us to speak clearly to Him about everything in our hearts, and He also wants us to listen.

Memory Verse Skit: (use Prayer Power Lesson 1, slide A)

Supplies needed: doctor puppet or doctor costume for skit

Doctor Word: Hi kids. I'm Doctor Word. I'm called that because I'm a doctor and because I love the Word of God. As a doctor, I use a lot of tools. One of the most important tools I use is a stethoscope. A stethoscope is one of the most powerful tools a doctor has because it amplifies sound. I can use it to check my patient's heart, lungs, and even listen to their stomach.

That reminds me of one of the most important power tools we have as Christians – prayer. That's why it's important to learn how to pray. When Jesus' disciples asked Him how to pray, He gave them an example of how to pray. It's called the Lord's Prayer, and it is our memory verse for this week.

In Matthew 6:9-13, Jesus said, "*Our Father in heaven, Hallowed be Your name. Your kingdom come. Your will be done On earth as it is in heaven. Give us this day our daily bread. And forgive us our debts, As we forgive our debtors. And do not lead us into temptation, But deliver us from the evil one. For Yours is the kingdom and the power and the glory forever. Amen.*"

Remember, tools don't work unless you use them, so let's decide to use our Prayer Power tool every day.

Offering:

Did you ever wonder why we pray over the offering before we take it? I did when I was younger. Then my teacher told me how we should pray over everything. Praying over the offering we give helps us to remember that God makes it more effective in the Kingdom of God. We should pray that God will use it for His glory. So, let's pray over the offering now.

Skit: Tyler the Power Tool Guy Doesn't Have the Tool He Needs

Supplies Needed: Tyler has a portable toolbox or toolbelt with various tools and is dressed in blue jeans and a plaid shirt, etc., power screwdriver. If you use a girl in the skit, have her dress the same and call her Tyler the Power Tool Gal.

(Tyler, the Power Tool Guy, comes into the room carrying an electric screwdriver. He plugs it in and starts revving it up.)

Leader: Excuse me, Sir. We're having children's church here, and you're interrupting.

Tyler the Power Tool Guy: (looks around like he just noticed everyone) Well, hello there. I'm as sorry as I can be for interrupting, but I have a work order to replace an outlet in this room.

Leader: Do you have to replace it now?

Tyler: I just do what they tell me. It will only take a moment. See, I have this power tool with different size bits. I just need to find the right one to unscrew the screws, and I'll be done in no time.

Leader: That is a nice screwdriver, but—

Tyler: Yes, it is. I got it at the Acme Power Tools Store. It has 6,000 different size bits, one for every kind of screw.

Leader: Don't you have to turn off the electric before you can change the outlet?

Tyler: Turn off the electric? Good idea. As soon as I find the right head for my screwdriver, I'll go do that.

Leader: Tyler, I'm going to have to insist you wait to change out the outlet. We're right in the middle of teaching these children. You can't turn off the electricity now.

Tyler: I'm powerful sorry, but this can't wait. As soon as I find the right bit, I'll have to turn off the power and change the outlet, but I'll be out of here in no time. (Starts looking through different bits. Distractedly asks question.) What are you teaching these kids?

Leader: I'm teaching them about spiritual power tools like prayer.

Tyler: Spiritual power tools. I don't have any of them. I thought I had every power tool there is. I'm going to have to go to Acme Power Tools Store and get me one of them.

Leader: You can't find prayer at a store. Prayer is talking to God. Today, we're teaching the children about the different components of prayer.

Tyler: Like different bits for a screwdriver?

Leader: Not exactly. With prayer, we have the ability to talk to God any time we want.

Tyler: Well, I'll get out of your hair as soon as I find the right bit for this screwdriver. I believe I need a Phillips Number Three. (rifles through screwdrivers) Oh no, 6,000 heads, and I don't have a Phillips Three. I need to go to Acme Power Tools Store and complain. (Packs up tools and leaves.)

Leader: Maybe Tyler, the Power Tool Guy, needs Prayer Power to help him find the right screwdriver head.

(Exits)

Verse of the Day: Matthew 6:9-13 (NKJV)

...Our Father in heaven, Hallowed be Your name.

Your kingdom come. Your will be done on earth as it is in heaven.

Give us this day our daily bread. And forgive us our debts, as we forgive our debtors.

And do not lead us into temptation, But deliver us from the evil one.

For Yours is the kingdom and the power and the glory forever. Amen.

Memory Verse Talk: Praise Sandwich (use Prayer Power Lesson 1, slide A)

Supplies needed: paper plate, bread, lunchmeat, lettuce, ketchup, mustard, and other sandwich elements, cheese

Did you ever wonder why people want you to memorize the Lord's prayer? After all, if prayer is just talking to God, why would we want to memorize a prayer. The importance of this prayer is not that we recite every word correctly. God doesn't want that kind of prayer. This prayer is a model for prayer. It helps us know how to pray. I'm going to illustrate this by making a praise sandwich.

First, we start with praising God. Place bread on the plate. *We'll use a slice of bread to show the praise.*

Then we let God know we want His will for our lives. This is one of the most important parts of prayer, so I'll use the lunchmeat to show God's will. Place a piece of lunch meat on the bread. *This is such an important part of the sandwich that I don't want to only use one slice.* Place two more slices of lunchmeat on the sandwich.

After that, we can start giving God our prayer requests. Everyone's prayer requests are different just as everyone likes different things on their sandwiches. Place each element on the sandwich as you talk about it. *Some people like lettuce. Others only want ketchup and mustard.*

The next part tops off the sandwich with something most people love – cheese. Place cheese on the sandwich. *When we pray, it's important to ask God to forgive us for anything we've done wrong and to ask God to help us forgive others. We don't only want God's forgiveness, though. We also want Him to help us do what's right and avoid what's evil. Just as cheese makes a sandwich better, this helps us live a better Christian life.*

This sandwich still needs something. Can you guess what it is? Have the children guess. If they don't guess bread right away, point to the bread to give them a hint. Place slice of bread on top.

A sandwich needs two slices of bread to make it easier to eat. And every prayer should start and end with praise. So, I guess you could say prayer is a praise sandwich.

Memory Verse Activity: Prayer Strips

Supplies needed: Marker board, chalk board, or blank wall; scotch tape; 1 set of strips of paper or poster board for each team with the following written on each sheet:

…Our Father in heaven, Hallowed be Your name.

Your kingdom come. Your will be done on earth as it is in heaven.

Give us this day our daily bread. And forgive us our debts, as we forgive our debtors.

And do not lead us into temptation, But deliver us from the evil one.

For Yours is the kingdom and the power and the glory forever. Amen.

Matthew 6:9-13 (NKJV)

Assign the children to teams. You can have up to six children on each team. When you say go, children from each team will arrange the lines of verse in order with the verse address at the end. They will tape the papers in order on the marker boards or walls. If you have a large group of students, you could have teams take turns doing this.

Bible Story: Jesus teaches His Disciples to Pray

(Matthew 6:5-14; Luke 11:1-4)

Supplies needed: marker board, poster, or projection device

If you could ask Jesus to teach you to do anything, what would you ask Him to teach you. If your students don't answer at first, make suggestions. Write down all the answers.

Jesus' disciples were always being taught by Him, but when they asked Jesus to teach them, what

9

do you think they asked for? The disciples asked Jesus to teach them to pray. Prayer must be very important if that's the one thing the disciples wanted to learn. Jesus taught the disciples this prayer, not because he wanted them to memorize it and recite it every time they prayed. The prayer was an example of things they could pray for. Let's look over the prayer again and think about the things Jesus told the disciples they could pray for.

... Our Father in heaven, Hallowed be Your name. Hallowed means honored or praised. So, Jesus wants us to start our prayers by praising God, our Heavenly Father. That's a great way to start a prayer.

Your kingdom come. Your will be done on earth as it is in heaven. Jesus wants us to pray for God's will to be done on the Earth. For instance, when you pray for your friend to know Jesus, you're praying for God's will to be done because God wants everyone to be saved.

Give us this day our daily bread. That's when we pray for the things we need and want. God is interested in our wants and desires as well as the things we need.

And forgive us our debts, as we forgive our debtors. If you have done anything God is not pleased with, this is the time to ask for forgiveness, but it's also the time to forgive anyone who has done something wrong to you.

And do not lead us into temptation, But deliver us from the evil one. We can't resist doing bad things on our own, but we can pray and ask God to help us do what's right.

For Yours is the kingdom and the power and the glory forever. Amen. This shows we end the prayer by praising God. Amen means "so be it". It's a way to show we have faith that God will answer our prayers. Now let's praise God.

Praise and Worship: Choose a couple of fast song and a slow song to lead children into praise and worship. It works well to talk to the children about what worship is and why it's important before you enter into this time. You can have a children's praise team, but until they understand leading praise and worship, have an adult leader or yourself be the worship leader.

Object Lessons:

1. 5 Finger Prayer

Supplies needed: none

Show how to use the fingers on your hand to illustrate how to remember the parts of the Lord's prayer.

Thumb - Praise

Our Father who is in heaven, Hallowed be Your name

The prayer starts out by praising God for who He is. Just as we can't do anything without our thumb, we can't do anything without God.

10

Pointer Finger - I Want What God Wants

Your kingdom come. Your will be done, On earth as it is in heaven.

Pointing your pointer finger toward Heaven, teach children to pray, "I want what God wants."

Middle Finger - Biggest Chunk of Prayer

Give us this day our daily bread.

Our third finger is our biggest finger, just like praying about our needs and the needs of others usually takes the longest time in prayer.

Ring Finger - Relationships

And forgive us our debts, as we also have forgiven our debtors.

The ring finger represents relationships. We ask God to forgive our sins so we have a right relationship with God. We ask Him to help us forgive those who have offended us so we have a right relationship with others.

Pinkie Finger – Small Problem

And do not lead us into temptation, but deliver us from evil.

Your pinky finger is your smallest finger. That's why we use it when we ask God to deliver us from temptation and the evil one. Compared to God, the devil is very small.

Fist – End with Praise and Power

For Yours is the kingdom and the power and the glory forever. Amen.

Just as we started with praise and worship, we end with praise and worship because God gives us power when we praise Him during our prayers.

2. Object Lesson: How to Pray

Supplies needed: none

You can illustrate this as a skit with 2 children or adults, or you can demonstrate it yourself. The examples come from Matthew 6 and Luke 18.

Jesus didn't only teach the disciples what to pray for. He also taught them how to pray. He taught them the attitude they should have when they pray. I'm going to give you some examples Jesus gave when he taught the disciples how to pray. See if you can figure out which one is the right way.

After each example is over, have your students guess which is the right way and tell why.

11

Example 1: Person one prays loud and uses a lot of thee's and thou's to impress. Person two prays humbly.

Example 2: Person one says the same thing over and over. You could use a rosary prayer or even the Lord's prayer, but have the person chant it many times. Person two praises God and asks Him to meet a certain need.

Example 3: Person one says, "Lord, I thank you I'm not like all of these sinners. Their robbers and bad people. I am a good person who gives in the offering, prays every day, and even fasts once a week. Person two says, "Lord, I am a sinner. Please forgive me."

Message: We Can Boldly Pray

Supplies Needed: rock, rubber snake, bread, toy fish

Sometimes, children have a hard time praying because they don't know how to pray. That's why we had this lesson about how to pray, but sometimes children worry about praying the wrong way, or they think they're not good enough to pray. That's not true. God wants us to talk to Him. He's always with us to help us through anything we might go through. He loves us. In the Bible, Jesus talks about how if we ask our parents for a fish sandwich (show fish), they won't give us a snake instead. (show snake) If we ask them for a piece of toast or bread, they won't give us a rock to eat instead. God loves us even more than our parents do. When we talk to God by praying, He wants to answer our prayers by giving us what is best for us. Even if we don't say the right words or remember all the ways to pray, we can still talk to God anytime we want to. He wants to hear from us.

For response time, encourage each student to separate from the others and find a place to pray privately.

Small Group Activity: Prayer List

Supplies needed: notebook or journal for each child, tabs to separate the notebook into the followed sections: praise, God's will, needs, forgiveness, protection

Give each child a notebook with tabs already labeled. These are their prayer journals. Explain how they can use these journals to write down their prayers and requests. Younger children can draw picture illustrating their prayers.

Tab 1 (Praise): Write down things we praise God for.

Tab 2 (God's Will): Write down prayer requests we know are God's will.

Tab 3 (Needs): Write down needs for us and others.

Tab 4 (Forgiveness): Write down things we need forgiven for and things we need to forgive others for.

Tab 5 (Protection): Write down temptations and situations we need protection from.

Give children time to write some of their prayer requests in their journals. Encourage them to put a star in front of each request as it is answered. Keep the prayer journals at the church until after the four lessons on prayer. Then the students can work on their journals each week.

Lesson 2 - Don't Worry - Pray!

Focus Point: When you are worried, pray about it.

Goal: Students will learn they can give their worries to God

Verse of the Day: Philippians 4:6 (ICB) *"Do not worry about anything. But pray and ask God for everything you need. And when you pray, always give thanks."*

Supplies Needed:

- doctor puppet or doctor costume for skit
- portable toolbox with various tools
- Tyler the Power Tool Guy Skit: Tyler wears a portable toolbox or toolbelt with various tools and is dressed in blue jeans and a plaid shirt, etc.
- power screwdriver
- post it notes or papers with scotch tape
- chairs in a circle
- Bible story: (optional) fake chains or ropes, toy swords, angel costume
- beanbag or soft ball
- backpack
- lots of heavy books, bricks, or rocks
- jar with lid
- pitcher with water
- dishwashing liquid
- food coloring
- tray
- vegetable oil
- 3 clear cups
- marker

Opening: *Power Tools Countdown* (optional) or *Power Tools* Slide

Welcome: Don't Worry - Pray

Supplies needed: post it notes or papers with scotch tape

Welcome children. I've been so worried about today's lesson, but then I remembered something very important. I don't have to worry about anything, because I can give my worries to God in prayer.

Ask the children for prayer requests. Write each prayer request on a separate piece of paper for game time later.

Prayer: Ask a child to pray over the service.

Rules: (use rules slide) Go over the 5 Ups Rules.

Go over the *5 Ups Rules*: 1. Sit up straight. 2. Listen up. 3. Hush up. 4. Don't get up and run around or go to the bathroom. 5. Worship Up! (stand up and participate during praise and worship)

Theme or Activity Songs: Choose one of two fast moving activity or theme songs that go with the curriculum.

Game Time: Musical Prayers (use game time slide)

Supplies needed: chairs in a circle, prayer needs from welcome time taped to the chairs. Have extra needs like children who don't have enough to eat or missionaries in case there aren't enough requests.

Play this game like musical chairs except make sure there are enough chairs for each student. When the music stops, have each student pray for the need taped to the chair he or she sat in.

Memory Verse Skit: (use Prayer Power Lesson 2, slide A)

Supplies needed: doctor puppet or doctor costume for skit

Doctor Word: Hi kids. I'm Doctor Word. I'm called that because I'm a doctor and because I love the Word of God. Being a doctor is a stressful job. I used to worry about all my patients, especially the ones who were very sick. I wouldn't be able to eat or sleep because I was so worried about them. Before long, I started getting stomach aches from the stress. That's when I read today's memory verse. Philippians 4:6 (ICB) says, *Do not worry about anything. But pray and ask God for everything you need. And when you pray, always give thanks.* After that, I stopped worrying about my patients. I would ask God to heal each of them and to give me the wisdom to treat their medical problems, and I would thank Him for answering my prayers. I started being able to eat and sleep again, and God would show me what to do with some of my patients. There were some patients He even miraculously healed without me having to treat them. I'm so glad I learned to stop worrying and to pray.

Offering: Treasures in Heaven (use Prayer Power Lesson 2, slide B)

Sometimes people call our money and possessions treasures. They call them that because they are valuable. God doesn't mind us having money and possessions, but He wants us to consider Him the most valuable thing in our lives. When we do that, we'll want to give in the offering to build the Kingdom of God. Matthew 6:21 (NIV) says, "For where your treasure is, there your heart will be also."

Have a child pray over the offering.

Skit: Tyler the Power Tool Guy Doesn't Have the Tool He Needs

Supplies needed: Tyler has a portable toolbox or toolbelt with various tools and is dressed in blue jeans and a plaid shirt, etc. If you use a girl in the skit, have her dress the same and call her Tyler the Power Tool Gal.

Tyler the Power Tool Guy: (Comes in muttering) What am I going to do? I just don't know what to do.

Leader: Hello, Tyler the Power Tool Guy. You look worried. Is anything wrong?

Tyler: Yes, something's wrong, and I just don't know what to do. If I don't get the outlet replaced soon, I'll probably lose my job. Then I won't be able to pay my rent, and I'll probably end up losing my apartment and living in my car. No, that won't work. I owe payments on my car too, so I'll probably be out living on the street in no time. Tyler, the Power Tool Guy, will be homeless. I never thought it would come to this.

Leader: Calm down, Tyler. Why can't you replace the outlet?

Tyler: I went to seven power tool stores. Not one of them has a Phillips Number Two bit for my power screwdriver. I need that attachment to replace the outlet. What am I going to do?

Leader: Your problem reminds me of our lesson today.

Tyler: You're teaching the kids how to replace an outlet. I can teach them that. That is if I had the right power tool.

Leader: I'm teaching these boys and girls what to do if they have a problem.

Tyler: Maybe I need that lesson because I sure have a problem.

Leader: The first part of the lesson is Don't Worry.

Tyler: Don't worry? That's easy for you to say. You don't need to replace an outlet when you don't have the right tools. You're not the one who's going to lose his job and become homeless.

Leader: Wait, Tyler. You don't understand. The most important part of the lesson is to pray. God knows what you need before you need it, and He knows how to help you.

Tyler: Just pray huh?

Leader: That's right. Don't worry – Pray.

Tyler: I'll try it. (bows his head and folds his hands together) Lord, I need to change the outlet box to keep my job, and I don't have a number two Phillips attachment for my electric screwdriver. Please, help me. (lifts head) Now what.

Leader: God will answer your prayer. Keep praying and thanking Him for the answer.

Tyler: That doesn't make any sense, but I'll try it. I don't know what else to do.

Leader: You'll see. Prayer works.

Tyler: I have to go now. I haven't tried Lowes or Home Depot yet. Maybe they have what I need. Even if they don't, I'll keep praying and try not to worry. Bye.

Verse of the Day: Philippians 4:6 (ICB) says, *Do not worry about anything. But pray and ask God for everything you need. And when you pray, always give thanks.*

Memory Verse Talk: (use Prayer Power Lesson 2, slide A)

Have you ever been worried about something? Worry is not a good feeling, but we all do it. Our memory verse for today tells us what to do if we're worried about something. It say's "Do not worry about anything." That's easy to say, but it's hard to do. Can you stop worrying just because someone tells you to stop. Allow children to answer. *I can't either. I'm glad the Scripture didn't just tell us not to worry. It tells us what to do instead.*

"But pray and ask God for everything you need. And when you pray, always give thanks." So, if I'm worried about something, instead of wringing my hands, dwelling on it, and worrying even more, I can pray and ask God for everything I need. Isn't it awesome that the God of the universe wants me to come to Him when I have a problem and tell Him what I need?

When I think about how much God cares about me, it's easy to do the next part of the verse. "And when you pray, always give thanks." Let's take a moment and give God thanks because He cares so much for us. Lead the children into a prayer of thanks.

Memory Verse Activity: (use Prayer Power Lesson 2, slide A)

Supplies needed: none

Have your students say the memory verse in different ways such as the following.

Whisper the verse.

Shout the verse.

Say the verse frightened.

Say the verse confidently.

Say the verse with a squeaky voice.

Sing the verse.

Bible Story: Peter Escapes from Prison

(Acts 12:1-17)

Supplies needed: (optional) fake chains or ropes, toy swords, angel costume

Tell the story in Acts 12:1-17. Have the children act out the story as you tell it with the following characters: Peter, King Herod, 1-4 soldiers depending on the size of your group, angel, Rhoda. All others depict the praying church. Tell the children what to do for each part of the story.

King Herod hated Christians. He even had James, one of the disciples, killed. Then he arrested Peter. Have King Herod order Peter be arrested. Have guards arrest Peter and chain him or bind him with ropes or chains. *Herod planned to kill Peter in the morning.*

Peter could have worried all night, but he trusted God to answer his prayers, so he went to sleep. Have Peter go to sleep in the middle of the guards.

The church was worried about Peter, so they had an all-night prayer meeting and prayed for Peter. Have the church say, "Lord, save Peter from Herod."

In the middle of the night, an angel appeared in the prison. Angel appears and says, "Peter, wake up." *Peter was so sound asleep that the angel had to shake him awake.* Angel shakes Peter. *The chain fell off Peter, and he followed the angel out of the prison.* Have Peter do so. *The guards didn't even notice.*

Once Peter was a couple of blocks away, the angel disappeared. Have the angel leave. *Peter was astonished because he thought he was dreaming.* Have Peter look surprised. *He decided to go to the house where the Christians were praying.* Peter walks around, and Christians say, "Lord rescue Peter."

Peter knocked on the door. Have Peter knock. *Rhoda, a girl who had been praying, answered it and was so surprised and overjoyed that she closed the door in Peter's face and went to tell the others Peter was outside.* Have Rhoda do so. *The church people were surprised too, but at first, they didn't believe Rhoda.* Have the church people say things like, "You're dreaming. Maybe it's his ghost."

Peter kept knocking, and eventually, Rhoda let him in. Then he told the people what happened.

Peter didn't worry. He prayed. The church worried about Peter getting killed, so they prayed instead of worrying. God answered their prayers and rescued Peter.

Praise Lesson: Beanbag of Thanksgiving

Supplies needed: beanbag or soft ball

The last part of our memory verse says, "And when you pray, always give thanks." We're going to take some time to do that. This is our beanbag (ball) or thanksgiving. I'm going to throw the beanbag. If you catch it, say something you are thankful to God for.

Throw the beanbag to as many children as you like. If you have enough students, give each of them a chance to catch the beanbag.

Praise and Worship: Choose a couple of fast song and a slow song to lead children into praise and worship. It works well to talk to the children about what worship is and why it's important before you enter into this time. You can have a children's praise team, but until they understand leading praise and worship, have an adult leader or yourself be the worship leader.

Object Lesson:

1. **Object Lesson: Let God Carry Your Burdens** (use Prayer Power Lesson 2, slide C)

Supplies needed: backpack; lots of heavy books, bricks, or rocks

Show slide and read the following verse.

Matthew 11:28 says, "Come to me, all you who are weary and burdened, and I will give you rest.

Choose the strongest boy in the class for this demonstration, or choose a teenager in the church to help you. Have him place the open backpack on his back. As you talk, continue to place heavy objects in the backpack.

There are many worries we carry in life. Even at your young age, worry is a part of life. For instance, you have to worry about homework and making good grades. Sometimes you might worry about making friends or having people like you. Some kids have to worry about moving away or their parents divorcing. Sometimes, there are even more things to worry about like someone abusing you or an illness you, your family, or a friend might have. Or you might have to deal with a bully who wants to beat you up or a teacher who doesn't like you. These are big worries. Even adults worry when things like these happen. These worries can weigh you down like this heavy backpack.

Ask the boy if the backpack is heavy. Ask him if he would like you to take away some of the weight.

Jesus cares about you so much, He wants to carry your burdens for you. That's what this verse is all about.

Instruct the boy to take off the backpack. Have him take each book, rock, or brick out and say, "Lord, I give this burden to you." After he has done that for each book, have him place the bookbag back on his back. Ask him if the backpack is lighter than before.

That's the way it is with each worry that burdens us down. As we pray and give that burden to God, He carries it for us because He care for us.

2. **Object Lesson: When Worry Bubbles Up**

Supplies needed: jar with lid, pitcher, water, dishwashing liquid, food coloring, tray

Preparation: Fill jar ¼ full with water. Fill pitcher completely with water and add food coloring. Place tray under jar to catch excess water.

Sometimes it's hard to stop worrying even when we do pray. Pour a good amount of dishwashing liquid in the jar and close with lid. Shake the jar vigorously while you are talking. The jar should fill with bubbles.

We might want to stop worrying. We might even pray about what we're worried about, but the more we think about it, the more worried we get. No matter what we do, we can't keep worry from bubbling up inside of us. Mention worries the students might have.

Nothing we do can get rid of the worry in our hearts. Open the jar and start to pour the colored water in the jar. *But if we ask the Holy Spirit to fill us with His peace and His joy and His love, He will take away the worry and fill us with the Holy Spirit.* Keep filling the jar until it overflows and there are no more bubbles left in the jar. *The more we are filled with God, the less worry we will have. When we pray, we want to not only give our worries to God, we want to ask Him to replace those worries with more of the Holy Spirit.*

Optional Video: Knock, Knock

Show **Knock, Knock** video found in Power Tools Additional Downloadable Resources

Matthew 7:7 (NIV) says, "Ask and it will be given to you; seek and you will find; knock and the door will be opened to you." Sometimes when we pray, it doesn't feel like God is answering us, but just as the man in the video did, God wants us to keep on asking, seeking, and knocking. He will answer our prayers.

Message: Worry and Prayer Don't Mix

(use Prayer Power Lesson 2, slides A & D)

Supplies needed: water, food coloring, vegetable oil, 3 clear cups, marker

Preparation: Use the marker to label cups worry, prayer, and Holy Spirit.

Mix food coloring with water and pour it in the first cup. *This cup represents worry.*

Pour oil in the second cup. *This cup represents prayer.*

Now let's see what happens when we combine worry and prayer. Pour both the water and the oil in the third cup. Wait a moment. Since water and oil don't mix, the oil will rise to the top above the water.

When we pray and give our worries to God in prayer, the Holy Spirit takes over and covers our worries. The more we pray and the closer we get to God, the more the Holy Spirit will cover us with His peace.

Show slide A. *Our memory verse, Philippians 4:6 (ICB), says, Do not worry about anything. But pray and ask God for everything you need. And when you pray, always give thanks. The next verse tells why we don't need to worry when we pray.*

Show slide D. *Philippians 4:7 (ICB) says, "And God's peace will keep your hearts and minds in Christ Jesus. The peace that God gives is so great that we cannot understand it."*

When we pray, the Holy Spirit covers our hearts and minds with His peace, peace so great we can't understand it. When that happens, we won't worry. Instead, we'll thank God. Worry and prayer don't mix when the Holy Spirit gives us His peace.

For response time, lay hands on each of your student's heads and pray for God's peace to overcome any worries they might have.

Small Group Chat: Send Worries to God

Supplies needed: helium filled balloons, ribbon, marker

Have a ribbon tied to each helium-filled balloon. Give each child a balloon and instruct that child to hold onto the ribbon until you say differently. Ask each child something he worries about and write it on that student's balloon. Abbreviate if you need to. Have extra balloons in case a balloon break or a student accidently lets go.

These balloons represent things we worry about. We're going to take the balloons outside. Hold onto the ribbon attached to your balloons. Don't let them go.

Take the students outside and have them stand in a circle.

Philippians 4:13 (ICB) says, "Do not worry about anything. But pray and ask God for everything you need. And when you pray, always give thanks." That's what we are going to do. Repeat after me. "Lord, take this worry from me. I give it to you." Now let go of the balloons.

Give your students a few moments to let the balloons float away. *Just as these balloons floated up to the sky, God will take our worries away when we pray, and He'll give us His peace.*

Lead your students in a prayer thanking God.

Lesson 3 - FAITH Prayers

Focus Point: Faith is the secret ingredient of prayer.

Goal: Students will learn they need to add faith to their prayers.

Verse of the Day: Matthew 17:20 (NIV) … *If you have faith as small as a mustard seed, you can say to this mountain, 'Move from here to there,' and it will move. Nothing will be impossible for you.*

Supplies Needed:

- doctor puppet or doctor costume for skit
- portable toolbox with various tools
- Tyler the Power Tool Guy Skit: Tyler wears a portable toolbox or toolbelt with various tools and is dressed in blue jeans and a plaid shirt, etc.
- power screwdriver
- balls or balloons
- mustard seeds (You can purchase these at any spice shop or in the spice section of the Grocery store. If you don't have a mustard seed, any small seed will do.)
- beanbag or soft ball
- Signs with the following written on them with a colorful marker: TIRED, EXCITED, JESUS IS HERE, BOO, THAT'S DIFFERENT, I WILL HEAL HIM, AMAZING
- Blindfold
- clear cup
- baking soda
- vinegar
- tray
- 2 Styrofoam or colored cups
- slush powder (available online or at magic shops)

Opening: *Power Tools Countdown* (optional) or *Power Tools* Slide

Welcome:

Welcome. I hope you've all been praying and writing prayer requests in your journals. Today, we're going to talk about the secret ingredient of prayer. What do you think that ingredient might be? Allow the children to answer, but don't comment on their answers. *Those were all good answers. One of them might have even been the correct one. But I can't tell you what it is. It's a secret.*

I'm just kidding. This is a secret God wants everyone to know. The secret ingredient of prayer is FAITH.

Prayer: Ask a child to pray over the service.

Rules: (use rules slide) Go over the 5 Ups Rules.

Go over the *5 Ups Rules*: 1. Sit up straight. 2. Listen up. 3. Hush up. 4. Don't get up and run around or go to the bathroom. 5. Worship Up! (stand up and participate during praise and worship)

Theme or Activity Songs: Choose one of two fast moving activity or theme songs that go with the curriculum.

Game Time: Ball Toss (use game time slide)

Supplies needed: balls or balloons

Have the students arrange themselves in a circle. The goal of the game is not to let any balls fall on the floor. Students will work together to keep the balls in the air. If a ball falls to the floor, the game is over although you can play the game more than once.

Start by throwing one ball into the circle. Once the students keep that ball in the air, throw in another ball. Keep throwing in balls, one at a time, until the game is over.

When the game is over, ask the students how difficult it was to keep the balls in the air when you kept throwing in more balls. This is almost impossible to keep up for long, but God does the impossible. That's why we can have faith in Him when we pray.

Memory Verse Skit: (use Prayer Power Lesson 3, slide A)

Supplies needed: doctor puppet or doctor costume for skit

Doctor Word: Hi kids. I'm Doctor Word. I'm called that because I'm a doctor and because I love the Word of God. Sometimes being a doctor and treating patients is almost impossible. That's even more true when a patient isn't getting better. I had a patient like that a couple of weeks ago. After doing all I could, I knew the patient was going to die of Covid. I used every medical technique I could think of, but nothing helped. That's when I read today's memory verse. Matthew 17:20 (NIV) says, *"If you have faith as small as a mustard seed, you can say to this mountain, 'Move from here to there,' and it will move. Nothing will be impossible for you."* I decided I wanted that kind of faith, so I spoke to the Covid virus invading my patient's body and told it to leave. I commanded my patient to be completely healed in Jesus' name. At first, nothing happened, but the next day when I was making rounds, I found out that my patient was completely better. He was miraculously healed and got to go home from the hospital that very day. From that point on, I knew faith is the secret ingredient that answers my prayers.

Offering: The Secret Ingredient of Giving

Whenever I give in the offering, I give in faith. First, I give knowing that God blesses me with money to give. Second, I know that God will use the money I give to build the Kingdom of God.

So, faith isn't only a secret ingredient for prayer, it's a secret ingredient for offering as well.

Skit: Tyler the Power Tool Guy Doesn't Have the Tool He Needs

Supplies Needed: Tyler has a portable toolbox or toolbelt with various tools and is dressed in blue jeans and a plaid shirt, etc. If you use a girl in the skit, have her dress the same and call her Tyler the Power Tool Gal.

Tyler the Power Tool Guy: (Comes in muttering) It didn't work. Now, I don't know what to do.

Leader: I don't understand. What didn't work?

Tyler: Prayer. I prayed God would help me find a Phillips number 2 bit for my power screwdriver, but it didn't work. I can't find the bit anywhere. I knew it wouldn't work before I even tried. Now, what am I going to do?

Leader: Wait a minute. Did you say you knew it wasn't going to work before you even tried praying?

Tyler: Yep, and I was right. Prayer is useless.

Leader: I agree.

Tyler: You do? But you're the one who wanted me to pray about it.

Leader: I'm not saying prayer is useless, but the way you prayed, you might as well have not even bothered.

Tyler: I don't get it. You mean there was a certain way I was supposed to pray?

Leader: That's right. There's a secret ingredient to prayer you didn't use. That's why your prayers didn't work.

Tyler: How in the world is that supposed to help me if it's a secret.

Leader: This is the kind of secret God wants everyone to know.

Tyler: I don't understand. If it's a secret, why would God want everyone to know?

Leader: That's a good question, but I don't have an answer.

Tyler: So, what's the secret?

Leader: Faith. Nothing is impossible for God, but we have to have faith that He'll answer our prayers.

Tyler: That won't help me. I just became a Christian a few weeks ago. I don't have a lot of faith like people who have been saved a long time.

Leader: You don't need a lot of faith. Matthew 17:20 (NIV) says, "If you have faith as small as a mustard seed, you can say to this mountain, 'Move from here to there,' and it will move. Nothing will be impossible for you."

Tyler: As small as a mustard seed? I saw a mustard seed once. It's really tiny.

Leader: Yes, it is. God doesn't require us to have this great big faith. He only wants us to have faith in Him. When we do that, we'll be amazed by what God will do. Nothing is impossible with Him.

Tyler: If I only need a tiny bit of faith, I'll try it. I have to go now. I want to try praying using my secret ingredient – faith.

(Exits)

Verse of the Day: Matthew 17:20 (NIV) … *If you have faith as small as a mustard seed, you can say to this mountain, 'Move from here to there,' and it will move. Nothing will be impossible for you.*

Memory Verse Talk: (use Prayer Power Lesson 3, slide A)

Supplies needed: mustard seed (If you don't have a mustard seed, any small seed will do.)

Matthew 17:20 (NIV) says, "If you have faith as small as a mustard seed, you can say to this mountain, 'Move from here to there,' and it will move. Nothing will be impossible for you." Have any of you ever seen a mustard seed? Show the mustard seed. *Mustard seeds are the smallest seeds there are. Why do you suppose God would want us to have faith as small as a mustard seed? I would think He would say, "If you have faith as big as a mountain, you can tell the mountain to be removed." But that's not what God says. Our faith only has to be a big as a mustard seed. God doesn't expect us to have some giant faith for our prayers to be answered. What He does want is for us to trust in Him. When we do that, He will answer our prayers in miraculous ways.*

Memory Verse Activity: If You...

If the following statements fit, students must stand and recite the verse:

Did you brush your teeth today?

Do you have blue eyes?

Do you have brown eyes?

Are you wearing green?

Are you wearing blue?

Did your parents drive you to church?

Come up with other questions until everyone has a chance, then make one more statement.

Do you have faith as big as a mustard seed? Encourage everyone to stand for this question.

Bible Story: Amazing Faith

(Luke 7:1-10)

Supplies Needed: Signs with the following written on them with a colorful marker: TIRED, EXCITED, JESUS IS HERE, BOO, THAT'S DIFFERENT, I WILL HEAL HIM, AMAZING. Write in pencil on the back what each sign says so you can easily find the right sign, or make duplicates of some of the signs so you can place them in order.

Show the signs as you tell the story. Instruct your students to say what the signs read with the feeling they convey.

A long time ago, after Jesus finished preaching to a large crowd of people, He came down from the mountain and headed to the town of Capernaum. Show TIRED sign.

News spread that Jesus was coming to Capernaum. Show EXCITED sign. *They were very excited. They knew Jesus had healed many sick people and had even raised people from the dead.*

They shouted, "Jesus is here." Jesus is here. Show JESUS IS HERE sign. *They shared the news with all of their friends. People filled the streets to try to get a glimpse of Him.*

Before long, a Roman centurion heard the news. Show BOO sign. *In that day, Romans suppressed the Jewish people and taxed them unfairly.* Show BOO sign. *They even took away their rights to be fairly treated.* Show BOO Sign. *This man wasn't only a Roman, he was a centurion, basically a captain in the Roman army.* Show BOO Sign.

But this centurion was different than most Romans. He love God and even donated money to build a synagogue, basically a Jewish church, for the people of that town. Show THAT'S DIFFERENT sign. *He even cared for his servants and treated them well.* Show THAT'S DIFFERENT sign. *One of his servants was sick. The centurion didn't want to leave his side, but he knew Jesus was the only one who could help the man. He sent for one of his officers and asked the man to send for the Jews who were the leaders of the synagogue he'd built.*

As soon as the leaders came to his house, the centurion said, "Go quickly and find Jesus. Beg Him to come and heal my servant." Most Jews wouldn't even go to a Roman's home, let alone help him, but because the leaders knew the centurion had helped them, did what he said. Show THAT'S DIFFERENT sign.

It wasn't easy for the men. They had to push their way through the crowded streets. Everyone in the town had flooded the streets saying, "Jesus is here." Show JESUS IS HERE sign. *Eventually the leaders found Jesus and pushed through the crowd to get near Him.* Show JESUS IS HERE sign.

27

They pleaded with Him to come with them and heal the centurion's dying servant. "If anyone deserves your help, it is this man," they said. "He loves the Jews and even paid personally to build us a synagogue."

I wonder if Jesus thought about how unusual it was for Jewish leaders to plead for a Roman centurion. Show THAT'S DIFFERENT sign. *I wonder if He was thinking about the sermon He'd just preached about loving your enemies.*

In any case, Jesus decided to go to the Roman centurion's house and heal his servant. Show I WILL HEAL HIM sign. *He followed the leaders of the synagogue through the crowded streets to the centurion's home. He probably had to push through the excited crowd to go there.* Show EXCITED sign.

When Jesus was almost to the centurion's home, a group of the centurion's friends arrived with a message for Jesus.

The message said, "Sir, do not trouble yourself to come to my home, for I am unworthy for you to enter under my roof or even to come and meet you. Just speak a word, and I know my dear servant will be healed." The Roman centurion had so much faith in Jesus that he didn't even need Him to come to his home. He knew Jesus would heal his servant. Show I WILL HEAL HIM sign.

The message also said, "I know how it is, for I receive orders from my superior officers and I give orders to those under my authority. All I have to say is, 'Go!' and they go, or 'Come!' and they come, and to my servant, 'Do this or that' and he does it. So if you just say, 'Be healed,' my servant will be made well." Show I WILL HEAL HIM sign.

When Jesus heard the centurion's words, he was amazed. Show AMAZING sign. *Jesus turned around and said to the crowd that was following Him, "Never among all the Jews in Israel have I met a man with faith like this."* Show AMAZING sign. *There's only one person in the Bible who amazed Jesus because of his faith. It wasn't one of His disciples or a Jewish leader. It was a Roman centurion.* Show THAT'S DIFFERENT sign.

After that, the centurion came to Jesus. Jesus turned to him and said, "Go your way. Just as you have believed, it will be done." Show I WILL HEAL HIM sign.

When the centurion and his friends returned to the house, they found the servant had been healed at the same time Jesus had promised.

I don't know about you, but I want to have the kind of faith that amazes Jesus. I want amazing faith. Show AMAZING sign.

Praise Lesson: Beanbag of Thanksgiving

Supplies needed: beanbag or soft ball

We're going to spend some time every week during this series thanking God. This is our beanbag (ball) or thanksgiving. I'm going to throw the beanbag. If you catch it, say something you are thankful to God for.

Throw the beanbag to as many children as you like. If you have enough students, give each of them a chance to catch the beanbag.

Praise and Worship: Choose a couple of fast song and a slow song to lead children into praise and worship. It works well to talk to the children about what worship is and why it's important before you enter into this time. You can have a children's praise team, but until they understand leading praise and worship, have an adult leader or yourself be the worship leader.

Object Lessons:

1. **What is Faith** (use Prayer Power Lesson 3, slide B)

Supplies needed: blindfold, obstacles

Sometimes, we hear a certain word, but we don't really know what it means. That is sometimes the case with faith, but the Bible tells us what faith means. Show slide and read verse. *Hebrews 11:1 (NIV) says, "Now faith is confidence in what we hope for and assurance about what we do not see." In other words, faith is the confidence we have in God before we see the proof. I'm going to give you an example of faith.*

Choose a student who is known for listening to instructions. Set up obstacles along the path you want the student to take. Have the student go to the back of the room. Blindfold him, and spin him around three times. Tell him that if he listens to your instructions and does them, no harm will come to him, and he'll make it to the front of the room.

Give the student instructions to avoid the obstacles and go to the front of the room. When he gets there, tell him to count slowly to three, then fall back. While he is counting, quietly stand behind him. When he falls back, catch him.

Congratulate the student in having enough faith to listen even when he didn't know you were there to catch him.

2. **Object Lesson: Faith That Pleases God**

(Use Prayer Power Lesson 3, slides C & D)

(Mark 9:17-27)

Supplies needed: clear cup, baking soda, vinegar, tray to catch excess water

Did you know that without faith, even your prayers won't please God?

Show slide C. *Hebrews 11:6 (NIV) says, "And without faith it is impossible to please God, because anyone who comes to him must believe that he exists and that he rewards those who earnestly seek him."*

29

God doesn't answer faithless prayers. So, if we have a hard time believing God will answer our prayers, how do we get enough faith to please God? One way is to ask God to give you faith.

Show slide D. *Hebrews 12:2 (ICB) says, "Let us look only to Jesus. He is the one who began our faith, and he makes our faith perfect."*

There was one man in the Bible during Jesus' time who was worried he didn't have enough faith. He was a father, and his son was tormented by demons who made the boy go into convulsions. The man had asked the disciples to heal the boy, but they couldn't. Then he went to Jesus and asked if Jesus could heal the boy. Jesus said, "Everything is possible for one who believes."

The boy's father knew he didn't have enough faith, but he said, "I believe. Help me overcome my unbelief." Because he asked Jesus to help him have more faith and overcome his unbelief, Jesus rebuked the demon, and the boy was healed. When we pray, we can ask God for the kind of faith that pleases Him.

Pour some baking soda in the clear cup. *Pretend this baking soda is a prayer that doesn't have the secret ingredient of faith. It just sits there and does nothing. Pretend this vinegar is faith. "Lord, please give me the faith I need to please you."* Pour in the vinegar. *God will give us the explosive faith that makes our prayers effective.*

Optional Object Lesson: Building Our Faith

Supplies needed: 2 Styrofoam or colored cups, slush powder (available online or at magic shops)

Preparation: Pour a tablespoon of slush powder into the first cup. Pour a little bit of water in the second cup. Try the experiment before doing it with your students to make sure you have enough slush powder.

Choose a volunteer. Ask the student if he or she trust you. If he says no, choose another volunteer. Have the student stretch out his hand and hold the cup with the slush powder. It is very important the student keeps his hand stretched out so he doesn't see what's in the cup.

Pour the water from the second cup into the first cup. Ask the student again if he trusts you. Tell the student to dump the water on his head. If he doesn't want to, encourage him to trust you. If he won't do it, ask for another volunteer. When the student dumps the water, nothing should come out. Take the cup away immediately so the student doesn't examine it.

Just as (student's name) trusted me when I asked him to do something he didn't want to do, we should have enough faith to trust God to do the impossible.

Message: Building My Faith

(Use Prayer Power Lesson 3, slides E-I)

Show slide E: *In the Book of Jude, the Bible tells us to build our faith. Here are some ways you can do that.*

Show slide F: *Ask God for faith. Remember that all faith starts with God, and He wants to give you the faith you need.*

Show slide G: *Remember that God does the impossible. With God, we can do anything even if our faith is only as big as a mustard seed. There is nothing impossible for God.*

Show slide H: *Learn God's Word. Romans 10:17 (NKJV) says, "So then faith comes by hearing, and hearing by the word of God." The more we learn about God from the Bible, the more faith we'll have.*

Show slide I: *Seek God: Hebrews 11:6 (NIV) says, And without faith it is impossible to please God, because anyone who comes to him must believe that he exists and that he rewards those who earnestly seek him." God doesn't want us to grow our faith for the sake of having great faith. It's more important to seek God than faith. As we seek God, our faith will grow.*

Small Group Chat: Mustard seed bookmark

Supplies needed: cardstock, glue, scissors, markers, stickers, colored pencils, mustard seeds (you can get them in any spice store or the spice department of your groceries store)

Preparation: Cut the blank cardstock paper in to bookmark size strips. For an 8 1/2 by 11 size paper, you should be able to make 5 bookmarks.

Have the children use the supplies to decorate their bookmarks. Encourage them to use mustard seeds as part of their decorations.

While the children are working on their bookmarks, tell a story about when God answered your prayer.

Lesson 4 - Powerful Prayer

Focus Point: Our prayers are powerful.

Goal: Students will learn they can change things through powerful prayers.

Verse of the Day: James 5: 16b (NIV) ... *The prayer of a righteous person is powerful and effective.*

Supplies Needed:

- doctor puppet or doctor costume for skit
- portable toolbox with various tools
- Tyler the Power Tool Guy Skit: Tyler wears a portable toolbox or toolbelt with various tools and is dressed in blue jeans and a plaid shirt, etc.
- power screwdriver
- screwdriver
- a package of cookies
- 12 rocks
- 12 small cups of water
- tray to catch water
- flash paper (available at magic shop or online stores)
- Alternative to flash paper (strips of red, orange, and yellow crepe paper, masking tape, scissors)
- beanbag or soft ball
- cellphone
- ornate lamp or bottle
- Optional - energy stick (available at Amazon, WalMart, and other stores)
- water
- food coloring
- vegetable oil
- 3 clear cups
- marker
- mustard seed
- Every Home for Christ World Prayer Map for Kids (Available free by mail from Every Home for Christ Ministries at https://everyhome.org/prayer/prayer-maps/)

Opening: *Power Tools Countdown* (optional) or *Power Tools* Slide

Welcome: Prayer Time

Welcome. For the last three weeks, we've been learning about the power of prayer. Today we're

going to talk more about powerful prayers. The best way to learn how to pray powerfully is to pray with your whole being. Sometimes, that means loudly. When I say go, I want you all to begin praying loudly for the next five minutes. I'll watch the clock and tell you when the five minutes is over. Go.

Prayer: Encourage children as they pray for five minutes. If they stop praying, give them suggestions for things to pray about.

Rules: (use rules slide) Go over the 5 Ups Rules.

Go over the *5 Ups Rules*: 1. Sit up straight. 2. Listen up. 3. Hush up. 4. Don't get up and run around or go to the bathroom. 5. Worship Up! (stand up and participate during praise and worship)

Theme or Activity Songs: Choose one of two fast moving activity or theme songs that go with the curriculum.

Game Time: Cookie Time Minute to Win It (use game time slide)

Supplies needed: a package of cookies, Minute to Win It Countdown found in Prayer Power downloadable resources

You might want to ask your students questions about the previous Prayer Power lessons to decide who participates, or if you have a smaller group, everyone could participate.

Explain to the students how the game is played. They'll each place the cookie on their foreheads. They have one minute to eat the cookie and can start when the countdown starts. Here's the catch. They can't use their hands. They have to use the muscles in their faces to get the cookie to their mouths to eat it. If anyone drops the cookie, he is eliminated.

It was almost impossible to eat that cookie in a minute without using your hands, but with God, all things are possible.

Memory Verse Skit: (use Prayer Power Lesson 4, slide A)

Supplies needed: doctor puppet or doctor costume for skit

Doctor Word: Hi kids. I'm Doctor Word. I'm called that because I'm a doctor and because I love the Word of God. Being a doctor is not for weaklings. When I was a resident, sometimes I had to work twenty-four hours at a time with very few breaks. Most of that time, I was on my feet. Then, when I became a doctor, I did full days of surgery. I would go from one surgery to the next with only a fifteen-minute break in between. You need power to be a good doctor. Prayer is the same way. Sometimes Christians believe that all God requires is a short prayer right before we go to bed, and everything will work out fine. While those short prayers are great, Christians who are effective in their prayers know how to pray passionately and powerfully. James 5: 16b (NIV) *"... The prayer of a righteous person is powerful and effective."*

Offering: Powerful Giving

Have you ever heard of powerful giving? In Luke 6:38 (NIV), it says, "Give, and it will be given to you. A good measure, pressed down, shaken together, and running over, will be poured into your lap. For with the measure you use, it will be measured to you." That's powerful. Whatever we give will explode and come back to us in the same measure or with the same power we gave. That doesn't always mean God will bless us with more money, but it does always mean God will bless us.

Skit: Tyler the Power Tool Guy's Prayers are Answered

Supplies Needed: Tyler has a portable toolbox or toolbelt with various tools and is dressed in blue jeans and a plaid shirt, etc. If you use a girl in the skit, have her dress the same and call her Tyler the Power Tool Gal.

Tyler the Power Tool Guy: (Comes in) I'm so happy you taught us about prayer for the last three weeks. Not only did I find out how to pray, but my prayers were answered and my job was saved.

Leader: That's awesome, Tyler. Tell us about it.

Tyler: I was so worried because I couldn't find a Phillip's number 2 bit for my power screwdriver, so I decided to pray. First, I asked God to help me find the bit, but that didn't happen. Then, I decided to pray in faith and power. I told God I didn't believe He wanted me to lose my job, but I couldn't find that bit anywhere. I asked Him to help me know what to do. Then I thanked Him for the answer knowing God wants what is best for me.

Leader: So, what happened?

Tyler: The next day, I went to the Acme Power Tools Store one more time because I believed God would answer my prayer. Usually, Acme Power Tools only sells power tools, but they were having a special sale. They had a display of regular screwdrivers in the front. I found a Phillip's number two and bought it. Not only that, but it was 50% off. I got it for much less than I expected to pay.

Leader: That's awesome. It sounds like your prayer was powerful.

Tyler: Yep. I took the tool to the church and replaced the outlet box in no time. My boss was happy I figured out what to do and even gave me a raise.

Leader: I'm so happy for you. So, are you going to change your name to Tyler the Tool Guy since you aren't using power tools?

Tyler: I wouldn't go that far. I still love my power tools. This was a one-time thing using a manual screwdriver, but I thank God, He showed me what to do. He is a powerful God who answers power prayers.

Leader: That's so true.

35

(Exits)

Verse of the Day: James 5: 16b (NIV) ... *The prayer of a righteous person is powerful and effective.*

Memory Verse Talk: (use Prayer Power Lesson 4, slide A)

Supplies needed: screwdriver

James 5:16b (NIV) says, "... The prayer of a righteous person is powerful and effective." I don't know about you, but I sure want my prayers to be effective. Effective means that something works right.

Show screwdriver. *For instance, this screwdriver is effective if it's the right size to remove a screw or attach it.*

But the verse goes farther. It says our prayers won't just be effective. They'll be powerful. Powerful means having great power or influence. We can pray powerful prayers when we understand that the God we are praying to is Omnipotent. Omnipotent means all powerful. It means nothing is more powerful than God.

There's one requirement in this verse for our prayers to be powerful and effective. Only the prayers of a righteous person are powerful and effective. Righteous means right with God, but nobody is righteous on their own. We are only righteous because Jesus died on the cross for our sins. We can't be righteous on our own. Only God can make us righteous. That means a person who doesn't believe in God or hasn't asked God to forgive their sins isn't righteous. That person's prayers aren't powerful or effective. I'm glad God makes my prayers powerful and effective.

Memory Verse Activity: Simon Says Verse

Have the students stand. Tell them you're going to play a game of Simon Says. If you say, "Simon says," they repeat what you say, but if you don't say, "Simon says," and they repeat it, they have to sit down. Say the first word of the verse. Then say the first and second word. Then say the first, second, and third word. Keep on going. When you are going to say the words correctly, say, "Simon says." Occasionally mess up the verse, but don't say "Simon says," when you plan to mess it up.

When the game is finished, tell everyone still standing that they won. It doesn't matter how many winners there are. The important thing is they all learn the verse.

Bible Story: Elijah and His Powerful Prayers (use Prayer Power Lesson 4, slide B)

(1 Kings 18:16-39)

Supplies Needed: 12 rocks, 12 small cups of water, tray to catch water, flash paper (available at magic shop or online stores), alternative to flash paper (strips of red, orange, and yellow crepe paper, masking tape, scissors)

Preparation for crepe paper fire: Cut strips of crepe paper. Tape on one end with masking tape.

(Show slide B) *James 5: 17 and 18 (NIV), the verses right after our memory verse, says, "Elijah was a human being, even as we are. He prayed earnestly that it would not rain, and it did not rain on the land for three and a half years. Again, he prayed, and the heavens gave rain, and the earth produced its crops."*

Even though Elijah was a normal person, it sounds like he prayed powerfully. Imagine being able to pray and stop the rain for three years, then being able to pray and start the rain back up. I'm going to tell you another powerful prayer Elijah made.

In those days, King Ahab and his wife, Jezebel, were evil. They encouraged the Jewish people to worship false gods. The people would go to the Temple and worship God, but they also worship the false gods. It's like Christian today who go to church on Sunday and worship God, but the rest of the week, they'll do things God isn't pleased with, or they'll go along with their teachers and friends and agree with things the Bible says are wrong. So Elijah's time wasn't that different than things today.

Elijah challenged King Ahab to a contest on Mount Carmel. He told the king to bring 450 prophets of Baal and 400 prophets of Asherah. That was 850 people on the king's side and Elijah on God's side In 2 Kings 18:21 (NIV), "Elijah went before the people and said, 'How long will you waver between two opinions? If the Lord is God, follow him; but if Baal is God, follow him.'"

Elijah then told the prophets of Baal to lay a sacrifice on an altar and he would do the same. He told them whoever called fire from Heaven to burn up the sacrifice, his God is the real God. He even told them they could go first.

The prophets of Baal and Asherah cried loudly for their gods to bring fire from Heaven until about Noon. When that didn't work, they cut themselves and danced around. By the time they were done, they were a bloody mess.

During all this time, Elijah mocked them. He would say things like, "Shout louder. Maybe your god is daydreaming, or maybe he took a long trip. Maybe he's asleep. Shout loud enough to wake him. Maybe he went to the bathroom. Maybe that's why he doesn't answer.

No matter what these prophets did, nothing happened.

Then Elijah said that it was his turn. He took twelve stones and built an altar. Place the 12 rocks on a table to build and altar. *Then he put the sacrifice on it, but that's not all he did. He told them to fill four buckets and pour them over the altar.* Pour four cups of water over the rocks. *Then he told them to pour four more buckets over the altar.* Pour four cups of water over the rocks. *They did so. A third time, he told them to pour four buckets over the altar, and they did.* Pour four cups of water over the rocks. *The water poured off the altar and filled the trench Elijah had dug.*

Then Elijah prayed a short, but powerful, prayer. He said in I Kings: 18:36-37 (NIV), "Lord, the

37

God of Abraham, Isaac and Israel, let it be known today that you are God in Israel and that I am your servant and have done all these things at your command. Answer me, Lord, answer me, so these people will know that you, Lord, are God, and that you are turning their hearts back again."

As you are saying this prayer, have fire come down from Heaven by lighting the flash paper or dropping the crepe paper fire.

The fire not only consumed the sacrifice, it caused the water to dry up. The people were amazed and fill on their faces crying out that the Lord is the real God.

Elijah trusted God and prayed, and God answered powerfully. We can pray powerfully when we understand that nothing is impossible with God.

Praise Lesson: Beanbag of Thanksgiving

Supplies needed: beanbag or soft ball

We're going to spend some time every week during this series thanking God. This is our beanbag (ball) or thanksgiving. I'm going to throw the beanbag. If you catch it, say something you are thankful to God for.

Throw the beanbag to as many children as you like. If you have enough students, give each of them a chance to catch the beanbag.

Praise and Worship: Choose a couple of fast song and a slow song to lead children into praise and worship. It works well to talk to the children about what worship is and why it's important before you enter into this time. You can have a children's praise team, but until they understand leading praise and worship, have an adult leader or yourself be the worship leader.

Object Lessons:

1. Pray With Confidence (use Prayer Power Lesson 4, slide C)

Supplies needed: cellphone

Show cellphone. *I use this phone when I want to talk to somebody. How many of you have a cellphone?* Have the students answer. *Who do you talk to on the cellphone?* Give the students a chance to answer. *Have you ever tried to call someone, but there wasn't enough reception to hear the person clearly?* Have the students answer.

Tell a story about when you needed to make an important call, but you didn't have any cell phone reception, or you phone died.

Show slide C. *1 John 5:14 (NIV) says, "And this is the confidence that we have toward him, that if we ask anything according to his will he hears us."*

That's an awesome promise. We can pray powerful prayers because we know God hears us.

We can have confidence that our phone line to God will always work.

2. **Object Lesson: God Always Answers** (use Prayer Power Lesson 4, slides D, E, and F)

Supplies needed: ornate lamp or bottle

Because we know God always answers our prayers, and because nothing is impossible with God, we can sometimes think of Him as a genie in a bottle. Show lamp or bottle. *We can get to a point where we use God to swoop in and give us whatever we want, then swoop out again. This is a dangerous way to think.*

Remember the Elijah story. God is all powerful. That's why the people who were playing around with worshipping God sometimes and worshipping other gods sometimes fell on their faces. They realized God is the real God, and we are not.

God wants us to pray and come to Him with our requests because He loves us. But whatever God decides to do, and however God decides to answer our prayer is always right because He is God.

We should also remember God doesn't answer every prayer. He only answers prayers prayed by His people, by Christians, but if we are a child of God, we can pray expecting God to answer us. Here are three ways He might answer.

Show slide D. *Sometimes God answers yes. He immediately gives us what we are praying for. This happened with Elijah when he prayed for fire to come down from Heaven.* Talk about a prayer in your life where God answered yes.

Show slide E. *Sometimes God answers no. We don't always know why God answers no. Sometimes He tells or shows us, but sometimes we won't know until we get to Heaven. If God says no, that's when we need to trust Him because He's God and we're not. In 2 Samuel 7, King David wanted to build a temple of God. God said no, not because He didn't love David or want the temple, but because He wanted King David's son, Solomon, to build it. King David helped Solomon plan the temple, but King Solomon built it.* Talk about a prayer you prayed where God said no.

Show slide F. *Sometimes God answers wait. There are times when God doesn't say yes or no. At those times, He is saying wait. It may be God plans to answer yes, but the time isn't right. Other times, He plans to answer yes, but He wants us to learn to be patient. Then there are times He plans to answer no because He is planning something better, and we don't know that until the better comes along. When the Jewish people were slaves of the Egyptians, they cried out to God for Him to rescue them. God didn't answer their prayers right away. Instead, He made them wait. During the waiting time, He was making Moses ready to become their deliverer.* Tell a time when you had to wait for a prayer to be answered.

Optional Object Lesson: The Power of Praying Together

Supplies needed: energy stick (available online at Amazon and other shops)

In Acts 2, God shows us that it is powerful when a group of believers pray together. Let me show you an illustration of that.

Have the students stand in a circle and hold hands except for two of the students. Hold one of those student's hands, and hold on the one end of the energy stick. Keep the circle broken for now.

God listens and answers our prayers when we pray alone, but when we pray in unity, our prayers become even more powerful. So, let's pray in unity. In a moment, I'm going to give you all something to pray for. If you stop praying, you must let go of the hands of the children next to you.

Give the children a need to pray for. Have the student not holding on to your hand grab hold of the other end of the prayer stick. It should light up. When a child breaks the circle, the stick will stop lighting up.

Just as power went through this energy stick when we were all in unity praying, our prayers are powerful when we all pray together for the same thing.

Message: Powerful Prayer

(Use Prayer Power Lesson 4, slides G-J)

Supplies needed: water, food coloring, vegetable oil, 3 clear cups, mustard seed

Today, we're going to review all the things we talked about in the last four Prayer Power lessons. All four of these things can make our prayers powerful.

Show slide G: The Lord's Prayer

Jesus gave us a pattern for praying. Show this pattern using this object lesson from Prayer Power Lesson 1.

Thumb - Praise

Our Father who is in heaven, Hallowed be Your name

The prayer starts out by praising God for who He is. Just as we can't do anything without our thumb, we can't do anything without God.

Pointer Finger - I Want What God Wants

Your kingdom come. Your will be done, On earth as it is in heaven.

Pointing your pointer finger toward Heaven, teach children to pray, "I want what God wants."

Middle Finger - Biggest Chunk of Prayer

Give us this day our daily bread.

Our third finger is our biggest finger, just like praying about our needs and the needs of others usually takes the longest time in prayer.

Ring Finger - Relationships

And forgive us our debts, as we also have forgiven our debtors.

The ring finger represents relationships. We ask God to forgive our sins so we have a right relationship with God. We ask Him to help us forgive those who have offended us so we have a right relationship with others.

Pinkie Finger – Small Problem

And do not lead us into temptation, but deliver us from evil.

Your pinky finger is your smallest finger. That's why we use it when we ask God to deliver us from temptation and the evil one. Compared to God, the devil is very small.

Fist – End with Praise and Power

For Yours is the kingdom and the power and the glory forever. Amen.

Just as we started with praise and worship, we end with praise and worship because God gives us power when we praise Him during our prayers.

Show slide H: Don't Worry, Pray

Redo Prayer Power Lesson 2 Object Lesson entitled Prayer and Worry Don't Mix found here.

Supplies needed: water, food coloring, vegetable oil, 3 clear cups, marker

Use marker to label cups worry, prayer, and Holy Spirit

Mix food coloring with water and pour it in the first cup. *This cup represents worry.*

Pour oil in the second cup. *This cup represents prayer.*

Now let's see what happens when we combine worry and prayer. Pour both the water and the oil in the third cup. Wait a moment. Since water and oil don't mix, the oil will rise to the top above the water.

When we pray and give our worries to God in prayer, the Holy Spirit takes over and covers our worries. The more we pray and the closer we get to God, the more the Holy Spirit will cover us with His peace.

Show slide I: The Secret Ingredient - Faith.

Supplies needed: mustard seed (If you don't have a mustard seed, any small seed will do.)

41

Show mustard seed. Then read Matthew 17:20.

Matthew 17:20 (NIV) says, "If you have faith as small as a mustard seed, you can say to this mountain, 'Move from here to there,' and it will move. Nothing will be impossible for you."

Show the mustard seed. Mustard seeds are the smallest seeds there are. Why do you suppose God would want us to have faith as small as a mustard seed? I would think He would say, "If you have faith as big as a mountain, you can tell the mountain to be removed." But that's not what God says. Our faith only has to be a big as a mustard seed. God doesn't expect us to have some giant faith for our prayers to be answered. What He does want is for us to trust in Him. Faith is the secret ingredient of prayer.

Show slide J: Pray Powerfully

Today, we learned that we can boldly come before God and pray powerfully. That's just what we're going to do now.

Response Time:

Have all the students come forward to the altar area. If you have a large group, split them up into sections of four to six students each. In each group, all of the students in that group will pray for each student one at a time. Instruct the students how to pray for each student in the group. Appoint one leader in each group to lay his hand on the student's head. The other students will place their hands on his back. Some students may want to give a prayer requests. If they don't, the other students can pray for God to bless that student and help him know God better.

Play worship music while the students are praying, and monitor the groups in case further instruction is needed.

If you don't have the small group chat, give each child an Every Home for Christ world prayer maps (free at this link - https://everyhome.org/prayer/prayer-maps/)

Small Group Chat: Powerful Prayers

Supplies needed: prayer journals, Every Home for Christ world prayer maps (free at this link - https://everyhome.org/prayer/prayer-maps/)

You can order free prayer maps from Every Home for Christ for each student at this link. https://everyhome.org/prayer/

Discuss what happened during prayer time. Have the students work in their prayer journals they started during lesson one to end the series on prayer.

ABOUT THE AUTHOR

Pastor Tamera Kraft has been a children's pastor for over thirty years. She is the director of a ministry called Revival Fire For Kids where she mentors other children's leaders, teaches workshops, and is a children's ministry consultant and children's revivalist. She is a recipient of the 2007 National Children's Leaders Association Shepherd's Cup for lifetime achievement in children's ministry.

You can find out more about Revival Fire for Kids at http://revivalfire4kids.net.